Editor
Melissa Hart, M.F.A.

Contributing Editor
Mara Ellen Guckian

Managing Editor
Ina Massler Levin, M.A.

Editor-in-Chief
Sharon Coan, M.S. Ed.

Cover Artist
Brenda DiAntonis

Art Coordinator
Kevin Barnes

Imaging
Rosa C. See
Ralph Olmedo, Jr.

Product Manager
Phil Garcia

Publishers
Rachelle Cracchiolo, M.S. Ed.
Mary Dupuy Smith, M.S. Ed.

Patriotic
Songs & Symbols
Grades 2–5

O say! can you ...
by the dawn's ...
What so proudly ...
at the twilight's last gleaming ...
Whose broad stripes and bright ...
stars, thro' the perilous fight,
O'er the rampa... 'tch'd,
...e so gallant...

We the People...

Written by

Melissa Hart, M.F.A.

**Teacher
Created
Materials**

Teacher Created Materials, Inc.
6421 Industry Way
Westminster, CA 92683
www.teachercreated.com
ISBN-0-7439-3599-3

©2002 Teacher Created Materials, Inc.
Made in U.S.A.

Table of Contents

Introduction to Teachers

Patriotic Songs and Symbols presents the histories and lyrics of eight songs which symbolize America's patriotism, courage, and desire for freedom. Numerous American symbols are explored, from flags to eagles to the different colored ribbons we wear on our clothing to indicate our support for a social cause. Students will learn that Katherine Lee Bates wrote the lyrics to "America the Beautiful," that Benjamin Franklin wanted our national bird to be the turkey instead of the bald eagle, and that "Yankee Doodle" was first sung by the British to make fun of American soldiers.

Activities are interspersed throughout this book. Students are given the opportunity to write their own pledges and patriotic songs. Exercises in designing symbols for money and stamps reinforce the idea of objects as representations of feelings about a place and its people. *Patriotic Songs and Symbols* provides activities across the curriculum. After reading about Johnny Appleseed, for example, students can follow a recipe to bake apples, and they can use the American flag to do simple math problems. They can learn to make their own instruments for a class parade and create a peace windsock. A final project asks them to make their own stationery and write letters to their congressperson.

In addition, this book provides many websites that students may use for further exploration of the songs and symbols that help to define the United States.

Flags of the U.S.A.

Directions: Look at the different flags that have been official flags of the United States. Color the flag in each box. Cut out the boxes, place them in the correct order, and staple them in the top left corner to make a mini-book.

U.S. Flags Mini-Book

Name_____

The Continental Colors (1776) **1**

The first Stars and Stripes (1777) **2**

The 26-star flag (1795) **3**

The 30-star flag (1848) **4**

The 36-star flag (1864) **5**

The 48-star flag (1912) **6**

The 50-star flag (1959) **7**

Honoring the Flag

The flag of the United States is a symbol to be treated with respect. Here are some rules for displaying the flag with honor. Cut out each of the boxes that hold the rules. Paste or glue them under the appropriate pictures.

Do not display the flag if the weather could damage it.	Do not hang the flag upside down. That signals a serious emergency.	Carefully fold the flag when it is not being displayed.
Do not let the flag touch the ground.	The flag of the United States may not be used for clothing. Use the colors, not the flag.	Display the flag from sunrise to sunset.

The Star-Spangled Banner

"The Star-Spangled Banner" was written on September 13, 1814, by 35-year old Francis Scott Key (1779–1843). It tells the story of the brave defense of Fort McHenry in Maryland against British attack.

Francis Scott Key was both a poet and a lawyer. He was opposed to war, but in 1813–1814, he served in the Georgetown Light Field Artillery. During this time, his friend, Dr. William Beanes, was taken prisoner by the British army. Key sailed on a truce ship to ask for his friend's return. On September 13, 1814, Key's boat stood eight miles below Fort McHenry. It was guarded by a British warship. From the deck, Key watched the bombardment of the American fort. Here, he became inspired to write the lyrics to "The Star-Spangled Banner."

In 1931, the United States Congress officially adopted "The Star-Spangled Banner" as the American National Anthem.

After you have read and discussed the words of "The Star-Spangled Banner" as a class, answer the questions below.

1. Define the following words from "The Star-Spangled Banner":

    perilous _____

    ramparts _____

    gallantly _____

    dread _____

    reposes _____

    fitfully _____

    desolation _____

    preserved _____

    motto _____

2. What is the star-spangled banner that Key wrote about?

    _____

3. Why were the British and the Americans fighting in 1814?

    _____

4. Who are the "free-men" that Francis Scott Key wrote about in the fourth stanza?

    _____

5. Why do you think "The Star-Spangled Banner" continues to be our national anthem?

    _____

The Star-Spangled Banner

by Francis Scott Key

O say, can you see, by the dawn's early light,
What so proudly we hail'd at the twilight's last gleaming?
Whose broad stripes and bright stars, thro' the perilous fight,
O'er the ramparts we watch'd, were so gallantly streaming?
And the rockets' red glare, the bombs bursting in air,
Gave proof thro' the night that our flag was still there.
O say, does that star-spangled banner yet wave
O'er the land of the free and the home of the brave?

On the shore dimly seen thro' the mists of the deep,
Where the foe's haughty host in dread silence reposes,
What is that which the breeze, o'er the towering steep,
As it fitfully blows, half conceals, half discloses?
Now it catches the gleam of the morning's first beam,
In full glory reflected, now shines on the stream:
'Tis the star-spangled banner: O, long may it wave
O'er the land of the free and the home of the brave!

And where is that band who so vauntingly swore
That the havoc of war and the battle's confusion,
A home and a country should leave us no more?
Their blood has wash'd out their foul footsteps' pollution.
Refuge could save the hireling and slave
From the terror of flight or the gloom of the grave:
And the star-spangled banner in triumph doth wave
O'er the land of the free and the home of the brave.

O thus be it ever when free-men shall stand
Between their lov'd home and the war's desolation;
Blest with vict'ry and peace, may the heav'n-rescued land
Praise the Pow'r that hath made and preserv'd us a nation!
Then conquer we must, when our cause it is just,
And this be our motto: In God is our trust!
And the star-spangled banner in triumph shall wave
O'er the land of the free and the home of the brave!

All About Fireworks

The creation of fireworks, sometimes known as pyrotechnics, is an ancient craft. Fireworks, when lighted, produce colorful lights, loud noises, and smoke. We set off fireworks on the Fourth of July to celebrate America's adoption of the Declaration of Independence on July 4, 1776.

Fireworks existed in China for centuries before their popularity spread to Europe. The Chinese made explosives as early as the 11th century. Historians believe Chinese gunpowder and rockets were brought to Europe in the 13th century.

Fireworks became very popular in Europe during the 14th century, about the time the gun was invented. Skilled military tradesmen, who were called firemakers, made shot and gunpowder. These firemakers created fireworks to celebrate victory or peace.

During the Renaissance, the Italians and the Germans worked hard to create new and different fireworks. Both groups added much to the development of pyrotechnics. By the mid-17th century, Europeans were setting off fireworks for all sorts of celebrations.

The United States discovered the thrill of fireworks in the mid-19th century. However, many children over the years have received injuries due to setting off fireworks improperly. Because of this, as well as danger of wildfires, the sale of fireworks is restricted by law in parts of the United States.

Most fireworks contain a substance such as potassium nitrate that supplies oxygen, plus substances such as charcoal and sulfur that combine with the oxygen which then produces heat and light. Sometimes types of starch, gums, sugar, shellac, and petroleum are used instead of charcoal and sulfur. The beautiful colors you see come from the addition of metal compounds.

Design Your Own Fireworks

If you were a firemaker, or pyrotechnician, what kind of fireworks would you design? Draw them on a separate sheet of paper.

U.S.A. Math

Name _____ Date _____

Directions: If your teacher wishes, you may use a calculator to find the answers to the following mathematical problems. Write your answers at the bottom of the page.

1. The flag of the United States has five rows with six stars each and four rows with five stars each. How many stars are on the flag of the United States?

2. The Declaration of Independence was approved on July 4, 1776. It said that the United States was no longer a part of Britain. How many years ago did the United States become free of Britain?

3. The United States made a law that the U.S. flag was to have 13 stars and 13 stripes for the 13 states. This law passed on June 14, 1777. Now June 14 is called Flag Day. How many years ago was the first Flag Day?

4. The first United States flag had 13 stars that stood for the original 13 colonies. How many more stars are on the United States flag now?

5. The Pledge of Allegiance was written by a man named Francis Bellamy in 1892. Congress made it a promise of loyalty to the United States in 1942. How long ago was it written?

6. The words for "The Star-Spangled Banner" were written as a poem by Francis Scott Key in 1814. He was happy because, even though the British were bombing Fort McHenry, in the morning the United States flag was still there. "The Star-Spangled Banner" became the national anthem in 1931 by an act of Congress. How many years after it was written did it become our national anthem?

1. _____   2. _____   3. _____   4. _____   5. _____   6. _____

You're a Grand Old Flag

George Michael Cohan (1878–1942) wrote the popular marching tune, "You're a Grand Old Flag." Cohan worked as a composer, playwright, actor, and producer. He first acted on stage at the age of nine. He presented his first play on Broadway in New York in 1901. Cohan wrote many patriotic songs in his lifetime. To see a photograph of him, go to the website below:

http://www.melodylane.net/standards4.html

After you have read and discussed the words of "You're a Grand Old Flag" as a class, answer the questions below.

1. Define the following words from "You're a Grand Old Flag":

   grand _____

   emblem _____

   boast _____

   brag _____

   acquaintance _____

2. Why do you think George Michael Cohan used the word "old" to describe the flag?

   _____

3. How does Cohan describe Americans in this song?

   _____

4. What does Cohan mean by "auld acquaintance"? What does he say we should do if we forget it?

   _____

5. Imagine you are asked to design a flag symbolizing your feelings about America. Draw your flag in the space on the right, and then explain why you chose this particular design.

   I chose this design for my flag because

   _____

You're a Grand Old Flag

by George Michael Cohan

You're a grand old flag,

　You're a high flying flag

And forever in peace may you wave.

You're the emblem of the land I love

The home of the free and the brave.

Ev'ry heart beats true

　'neath the Red, White, and Blue,

Where there's never a boast or brag.

Should auld acquaintance be forgot,

Keep your eye on the grand old flag.

The Pledge of Allegiance

The Pledge of Allegiance to the United States Flag symbolizes our loyalty to America. Francis Bellamy (1855-1931), a Baptist minister, wrote the original Pledge in August 1892. It was published in a children's magazine called *The Youth's Companion*. More than 12 million children first recited the Pledge on October 12, 1892, during school celebrations of Columbus Day.

The Pledge of Allegiance was officially recognized by the United States Congress in 1942.

When people recite the Pledge, they usually put their right hands over their hearts. Men should remove their hats. People who work in the military give the military salute.

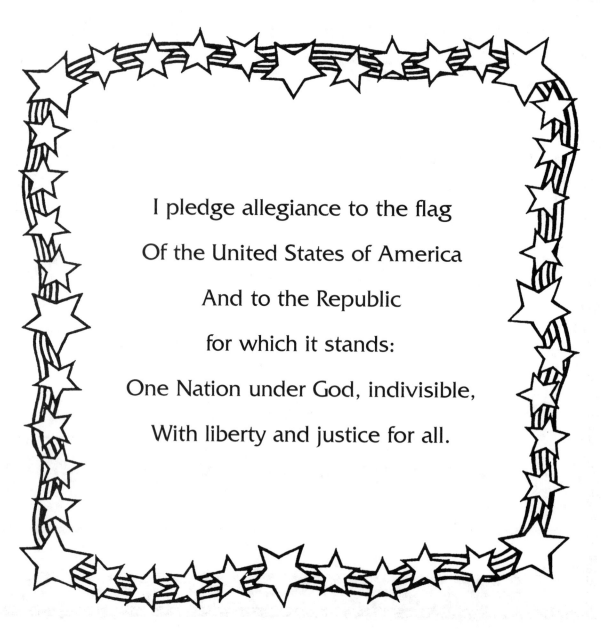

I pledge allegiance to the flag

Of the United States of America

And to the Republic

for which it stands:

One Nation under God, indivisible,

With liberty and justice for all.

Write Your Own Pledge

A pledge is a promise that you make to someone. In the space below, write your own pledge. It might be a promise to a parent, a sister or brother, or a friend. You might make a pledge to a favorite pet or to the land in which you live. Be creative and have fun!

_____

_____

_____

_____

_____

_____

_____

_____

_____

_____

_____

_____

_____

_____

_____

_____

The *Mayflower*

When people talk about the first ships that carried settlers from England to the United States, they usually mention the *Mayflower*. The *Mayflower* began its journey across the Atlantic in 1620. Approximately 102 passengers traveled on this small ship. Half of the travelers were Pilgrims. The others were soldiers and other British settlers. Some Americans can trace their ancestors all the way back to those people who first traveled on the *Mayflower*.

It took the *Mayflower* three months to make the trip from England to America. The ship was headed for Virginia, but because of stormy weather and errors in direction, it landed in Provincetown, Massachusetts. During the journey, a group of men on the ship decided to write the "Mayflower Compact." This was a written promise that they would all work together in America and obey the rules that they made as a group. All adult males on the boat had to sign this agreement. The authors were certain that without such a promise, settlers would die.

The settlers founded Plymouth Colony, the first permanent settlement in New England. They used the Mayflower Compact to keep order in the new land. But there was nothing the Compact could do about the cold and illness that afflicted the settlers. About half of the passengers from the *Mayflower* died from illness during their first winter in America.

The *Mayflower* is remembered as a symbol of the cooperation, courage, and faith that helped new Americans to survive in a strange and frightening land.

Writing Assignment

Pretend you have just stepped off the *Mayflower* onto American land. Write a letter to a friend back in England describing how you feel, what you see, and your memories of the long trip across the Atlantic by ship.

The Statue of Liberty and Ellis Island

The Statue of Liberty is a symbol of international freedom. It was created to celebrate the friendship between France and the United States during the American Revolution (1775–1783). The statue was designed by French sculptor Frédéric-Auguste Bartholdi. The iron frame was created by French engineer Gustave Alexandre Eiffel—the same man who built the Eiffel Tower in Paris. The French people donated the money for the statue itself, which was first exhibited in Paris before being shipped to America. The pedestal was designed by American architect Richard Morris Hunt.

The Statue of Liberty is located on Liberty Island in New York City. It was dedicated by United States President Grover Cleveland on October 28, 1886, and proclaimed a national monument in 1924. The Statue of Liberty was often the first thing that thousands of visitors and immigrants saw as they approached America by ship for the first time.

The Statue's formal name is Liberty Enlightening the World. It depicts a woman escaping from chains, which lie at her feet. The chains symbolize persecution. Her right hand holds a burning torch that represents liberty. Her left hand holds a tablet inscribed with the date "July 4, 1776," the day the United States declared its independence from Britain. The seven rays of her spiked crown symbolize the seven seas and continents.

The Statue of Liberty is 151 feet (46 m) high. The base and pedestal increase its height to 305 feet (93 m). Ferries from Battery Park in New York City take visitors to Liberty Island. Visitors can climb 192 steps to an observation area and museum at the top of the pedestal. The full climb of 354 steps takes visitors from the pedestal to Liberty's crown. Here they can look out over New York Harbor and the city.

America the Beautiful

Katharine Lee Bates (1859–1929) first saw Pike's Peak, a 14,000 foot mountain in Colorado, in 1883. The majestic view inspired her to write the popular patriotic song "America the Beautiful."

Katharine Lee Bates was born in 1859 in Falmouth, Massachusetts where she grew up. She attended and graduated from Wellesley College in Massachusetts. Later, she taught there and worked as head of the English department. She wrote travel books, textbooks, children's books, and short stories before writing the poem that became "America the Beautiful." The poem appeared two years later in the *Congregationalist Newspaper*. Later, it was published in the *Boston Evening Transcript*. Bates didn't write the poem intending it to be sung, but its rhythm so perfectly fit a tune called "Materna" by Samuel Augustus Ward that soon our nation was humming "America the Beautiful" almost as often as "The Star-Spangled Banner"!

After you have read and discussed the words of "America the Beautiful" as a class, answer the questions below.

1. Define the following words from "America the Beautiful":

   spacious _____

   amber _____

   brotherhood_____

   impassioned _____

   thoroughfare _____

   liberating _____

   strife _____

   divine_____

   patriot _____

   alabaster _____

2. What is the "fruited plain" that Bates refers to in the first stanza of "America the Beautiful"?

   _____

3. Bates admires Pilgrims in the second stanza. How did this group of people fight for American freedom?

   _____

4. Who are the heroes that Bates writes about in the third stanza? Why does she consider them heroes?

   _____

America the Beautiful

by Katharine Lee Bates

O beautiful for spacious skies,
For amber waves of grain,
For purple mountain majesties
Above the fruited plain!

Chorus
America! America!
God shed his grace on thee
And crown thy good with brotherhood
From sea to shining sea!

O beautiful for pilgrim feet
Whose stern impassioned stress
A thoroughfare for freedom beat
Across the wilderness!

America! America!
God mend thine ev'ry flaw,
Confirm the soul in self control,
Thy liberty in law!

O beautiful for heroes proved
In liberating strife.
Who more than self their country loved
And mercy more than life!

America! America!
May God thy gold refine
Till all success be nobleness
And every gain divine!

O beautiful for patriot dream
That sees beyond the years
Thine alabaster cities gleam,
Undimmed by human tears!

Repeat Chorus

The Liberty Bell

The Liberty Bell symbolizes American freedom from British rule. It was rung on July 8, 1776, in Philadelphia after the first public reading of the Declaration of Independence. The bell weighs 2080 pounds (943.5 kg) and its circumference is 12 feet (3.7 m).

The bell was ordered for the United States in 1751. Ironically, it was cast in London. It arrived in Philadelphia in August 1752 and was cracked while being tested. It was melted down, and a second bell was cast in April 1753. However, this bell also had flaws. A third was cast in June of that year. On June 7, 1753, the third bell was hung in the tower of Independence Hall.

In 1777, during the American Revolution, British troops occupied Philadelphia. Concerned Americans removed the bell from the tower and took it to Allentown, Pennsylvania, where they felt it would be safer. A year later, it was returned to Philadelphia and replaced in Independence Hall.

The Liberty Bell was rung on every Fourth of July and during every state celebration until 1835. That year, it cracked as it was being rung for the death of Chief Justice John Marshall. The Liberty Bell now hangs in a glass pavilion near Independence Hall.

Fast Facts

Answer the following questions based on the information above:

1. How much does the Liberty Bell weigh?

_____

2. Where was it first cast?

_____

3. Why was it recast in 1753?

_____

4. When did the Liberty Bell crack?

_____

5. Where can you go to see the Liberty Bell now?

_____

Daily Journal Topics

1. Katharine Lee Bates wrote "America the Beautiful" after seeing the Colorado mountains. What place in America is the most beautiful to you? Describe it in your journal.

2. Write a description of what America means to you. What does America smell like, taste like, look like? What does it feel like? What does it sound like?

3. Write about your neighborhood—your own small piece of America. Describe the people, buildings, plants, and animals that make your neighborhood unique.

4. Pretend that you are the Statue of Liberty. Write a story describing what you observe about the immigrants who arrive at Ellis Island and see the United States for the first time. What do they look like? What do they say? How do they feel about coming to a new country?

5. Write a letter to someone in a different part of the United States. Describe your part of the country for that person so that he or she understands what it's like to live there. Include details about the land, the weather, the people, and the animals in your location.

America

Reverend Samuel Francis Smith was busy translating a German patriotic hymn in order to make some much-needed money in his last year of seminary school. Then, he decided that the United States needed a national poem. He wrote this poem, which he titled "America," on scraps of paper. His friend, a musician named Lowell Mason, published it. "America" was first sung at a children's Sunday school celebration of American freedom in Boston, on July 4, 1832.

The tune that Smith set his poem to is popular among other nations, as well. England uses the tune for its anthem, "God Save the Queen." Nine years after Smith adopted it for "America," Beethoven wrote piano variations on the tune.

Smith wrote over 150 hymns during his lifetime. Later, he traveled with the Baptist Missionary Union. He could speak 15 different languages! When he was 86 years old, he tried to learn one more language—Russian—before he died.

After you have read and discussed the words of "America" as a class, answer the questions below.

1. Define the following words from "America":

   native _____

   noble _____

   rills _____

   rapture _____

   mortal _____

   partake _____

   prolong _____

2. Smith writes that his "fathers" died in America. Which men is Reverend Smith referring to?

   _____

3. What details does Smith love about the American landscape?

   _____

4. What is Smith suggesting that we should do in the third stanza of "America"?

   _____

America

by Samuel Francis Smith

My country, 'tis of thee,
Sweet land of liberty,
Of thee I sing;
Land where my fathers died,
Land of the Pilgrim's pride,
From every mountainside
Let freedom ring.

My native country, thee,
Land of the noble free,
Thy name I love;
I love thy rocks and rills,
Thy woods and templed hills;
My heart with rapture thrills
Like that above.

Let music swell the breeze,
And ring from all the trees
Sweet freedom's song;
Let mortal tongues awake;
Let all that breathe partake,
Let rocks their silence break,
The sound prolong.

Our fathers' God to, thee,
Author of liberty,
To Thee we sing;
Long may our land be bright
With freedom's holy light;
Protect us by Thy might,
Great God, our King.

The Bald Eagle and the Great Seal of the United States

The Great Seal of the United States was created shortly after the signing of the Declaration of Independence on July 4, 1776. A committee made up of Benjamin Franklin, John Adams, and Thomas Jefferson submitted an idea for the seal. However, the Continental Congress found their design unacceptable. Charles Thomson eventually had the honor of designing what would become the official Seal of the United States.

The bald eagle was suggested as America's national symbol on June 20, 1782, the date that the Seal was adopted. As the story goes, one morning during the American Revolution, the sounds of battle startled a nest of bald eagles. The majestic birds circled over the heads of the soldiers, shrieking all the while. "They're crying for freedom!" said the patriots.

The bald eagle symbolizes courage, strength, and freedom—the same ideals upon which America was founded. However, many people felt that the bird was not an appropriate symbol for the United States. Benjamin Franklin wrote a letter suggesting that the turkey would be a far better choice to represent the true essence of America. He said that bald eagles were cowards because they stole fish from other birds and flew away when attacked by much smaller kingbirds.

By this time, several states had already used the bald eagle in their coat of arms. Later, the eagle appeared on United States coins, paper money, and stamps.

The bald eagle is depicted on the Great Seal of the United States of America. It holds a bundle of arrows in one of its talons to symbolize war and an olive branch in the other to symbolize peace. In its beak, it holds a banner reading "E Pluribus Unum," which is Latin for "Out of many, one." The other side of the Seal depicts a pyramid with an eye—the eye of Divine Providence—on top. The base of the pyramid is inscribed with the year 1776 in Roman numerals.

The Democratic Donkey
and the Republican Elephant

When Andrew Jackson ran for president of the United States in 1828, some people felt he acted like a donkey because of his stubborn political views. Jackson was so amused by their words that he started putting pictures of donkeys on his campaign posters. In 1870, political cartoonist Thomas Nast drew donkeys to symbolize Democratic editors and newspapers. The donkey quickly became an unofficial mascot representing the Democratic Party. Democrats like to say that the donkey, like their political party, is courageous, smart, and lovable.

Nast was also responsible for making the elephant the symbol of the Republican Party. He drew a cartoon of an elephant running away from à donkey in an 1874 issue of the magazine *Harper's Weekly*. The Republicans officially adopted the elephant as their party's symbol, claiming that it shows great dignity, intelligence, and strength.

Design Your Own Symbolic Animal

What animal would make a good symbol for you? In the space below, draw a picture of your animal, and then write a few sentences explaining why it symbolizes you.

We Shall Overcome

Early African-American music grew out of the experiences of slaves brought over to the United States from Africa. The songs and spirituals that developed over time brought slaves a sense of hope during their difficult workdays. The songs also gave people a way to communicate with each other while working. Sometimes, the songs contained coded information so that slaves could secretly communicate without being punished by slaveholders. These songs provided them with rhythms to pace themselves as they picked cotton or hoed fields. Spirituals were often sung in praise of God, as these slaves looked toward a future free of captivity.

Often, more than one person wrote these songs and spirituals. Many songs, such as "We Shall Overcome," used the African call-and-response style. A leader would introduce the line of a melody, and other singers would chime in with the chorus.

The first known references to African-American spirituals date from approximately 1819. Their rhythms and melodies are much like songs from West Africa. Many times, these songs and spirituals were accompanied by clapping, snapping, and foot tapping.

Writing Assignment

African Americans have made amazing contributions to the United States in fields such as science, the arts, sports, and politics. Research one African-American person on the website

http://www.uga.edu/~iaas/History.html

Write a one-page report describing this person and what he or she has contributed to America.

We Shall Overcome

by *Anonymous*

We shall overcome.
We shall overcome.
We shall overcome some day.

Chorus

Oh, deep in my heart
I do believe
We shall overcome some day.

We'll walk hand in hand.
We'll walk hand in hand.
We'll walk hand in hand some day.

Chorus

We shall all be free,
We shall all be free,
We shall all be free some day.

Chorus

We shall live in peace,
We shall live in peace,
We shall live in peace some day.

Chorus

The Native American Peace Pipe and the Buffalo

The Peace Pipe

Today, people talk about "smoking a peace pipe" to symbolize cooperation between people worldwide. In previous centuries, however, the peace pipe represented good relationships between the different nations of Native Americans. Important members of the tribes would gather in a circle, where an elder chief would hold up a clay pipe. This pipe was usually decorated with feathers and beads. He would fill the bowl of the pipe with tobacco and say a prayer to the great spirits. Then he would sing a special song and put a live coal from the fire on the bowl to light the pipe.

Once the peace pipe was lit, the leader would point the pipe north, south, east, west, toward the sky, and toward the earth. He did this as an offering to the spirits. Then he would pass the pipe to other people in the circle. They would repeat his ritual. Native Americans passed the pipe around a circle to create a feeling of unity. They believed that the smoke drifting upward made communication with the spirit world easier.

The Buffalo

The buffalo, or bison, symbolized life to many Native American nations. It provided them with all of their needs, including food, clothing, and shelter made from the buffalo's hide, fuel from its droppings, and weapons from its horns.

The buffalo appears on the seal of the United States Department of the Interior. The buffalo nickel was designed in 1913. Its makers wanted to create a coin that no other country would have. The buffalo was the most American symbol they could imagine.

The buffalo population dropped from 15 million in the year 1880 to only 500 in 1885. Settlers from the East wanted the Native Americans' land. They felt that the best way to get it would be to destroy the buffalo that these people depended on. The United States now operates buffalo preserves in an effort to reintroduce this animal to the western prairie.

Smokey the Bear

A huge forest fire raged in the New Mexico forest in the 1950s, destroying 17,000 acres. An American black bear cub found himself surrounded by flames. He climbed up a burnt tree to escape getting killed. It was here that firefighters found the badly burned and hungry cub. They admired him for his courage and will to survive. They couldn't find his mother, so the firefighters sent the bear cub to live at the National Zoo in Washington, D.C. In 1961, another bear found in New Mexico became Smokey's friend. Her name was Goldie, and she lived with Smokey until he died in 1976.

The cartoon version of Smokey the Bear was created in 1944 by an artist named Albert Stehle. Smokey symbolizes the importance of preventing forest fires. More than half of these fires are caused by humans. There are over 700 million acres of forests in the United States. These forests provide shade, food, and shelter for wildlife. They also produce oxygen, which we all must have to breathe!

One of the biggest dangers to a forest is fire. Fire destroys the homes of animals, birds, and people. For fifty years, Smokey the Bear has been asking children not to play with matches or other flammable objects which could start a fire. "Only you can prevent forest fires," he says.

Smokey the Bear is usually shown wearing blue jeans, a belt, and a hat with his name on it. He often holds a shovel. The shovel symbolizes one of the rules of making a safe campfire. To find out the rest of the rules, go to the website below:

http://www.smokeybear.com/cam_main.html

Forest Fire Questions

1. Name two actions that Smokey suggests people take in order to prevent wildfires. _____

   _____

2. Write the rules that Smokey says we should follow when making a campfire.

   _____

   Feel free to explore the rest of Smokey's website. You can play games, see photos of a real American black bear, and even write a letter to Smokey!

Write Your Own Patriotic Song

What does America mean to you? In the space below, write a song about your feelings for the United States. Here are a few words to get you started:

- Freedom
- Peace
- Eagle
- Stars and Stripes
- Beauty
- Opportunity
- Pilgrim
- Pride
- Patriotic
- Flag
- Land
- Liberty

Uncle Sam

No one knows exactly who Uncle Sam was or how he came to be a symbol of United States patriotism. He is usually shown wearing a beard and a tall hat decorated with stars and stripes. His pants are striped red and white, and he wears a blue coat.

In 1813, a New York newspaper reported that the owner of a meat-processing plant, Sam Wilson, began stamping the meat sold to the United States Army with the letters U.S. Some people said that the initials stood for United States. Other people said they stood for Uncle Sam, which is what the workers at the processing plant called Wilson.

Whatever the initials stood for, the nickname caught on. People began to refer to anything belonging to the United States government as "Uncle Sam's." Political cartoonists began drawing pictures of a man dressed like the American flag. The military put him on their posters to recruit soldiers for World War I and World War II. To see one of the posters, search on Encarta or go to the following website:

http://home.nycap.rr.com/content/us_poster_l.jpg

In 1961, the United States Congress adopted Uncle Sam as a national symbol. He has become part of American vocabulary. "I'm working for Uncle Sam," you might hear someone say, or "Uncle Sam is helping me to put my kids through college."

When Johnny Comes Marching Home

Patrick Sarsfield Gilmore was born on Christmas Day in 1829 in Ireland. When he was still a young boy, he accompanied his father to a protest rally as a member of the Ballygar Fife and Drum Band. He loved the experience so much that he decided to devote his life to music. In 1848, Gilmore and his brother immigrated from Ireland to Boston. He became the leader of the Boston Brigade Band, and later, the Charlestown Band. He was known as the best trumpet player in the eastern United States.

Gilmore, along with his band from Salem, Massachusetts, played at many military functions during the Civil War. He was also asked to train other military bands. At the end of the war, Abraham Lincoln asked Gilmore to gather together as many musicians as possible for a celebration in New Orleans. He came up with 500 musicians and 5,000 schoolchildren to perform patriotic songs. He used a cannon to accompany the band. This celebration so inspired Gilmore that he organized even larger groups of musicians to perform musical celebrations. On New Year's Eve, 1888, Gilmore started a tradition in Times Square in New York City that continues to this day. His band played for the crowd, and then he himself fired two pistols to welcome in the new year.

Gilmore wrote several famous patriotic songs, among them: "John Brown's Body," "Good News from Home," "God Save Our Nation," and "When Johnny Comes Marching Home." This last song was playing as American troops walked off the planes after fighting in Operation Desert Storm in 1991.

After you have read and discussed the words of "When Johnny Comes Marching Home" as a class, answer the questions below.

1. Define the following words from "When Johnny Comes Marching Home":

    hearty _____

    peal _____

    lads_____

    lassies _____

    strew_____

    jubilee_____

    laurel _____

    choicest _____

2. Who does "Johnny" symbolize?

    _____

3. Why are people so happy to see Johnny come marching home?

    _____

4. What types of things will people do to welcome Johnny home?

    _____

When Johnny Comes Marching Home

by Patrick Sarsfield Gilmore

When Johnny comes marching home again,
Hurrah! Hurrah!
We'll give him a hearty welcome then
Hurrah! Hurrah!
The men will cheer and the boys will shout
The ladies they will all turn out

Chorus
And we'll all feel gay,
When Johnny comes marching home.

The old church bell will peal with joy
Hurrah! Hurrah!
To welcome home our darling boy
Hurrah! Hurrah!
The village lads and lassies say
With roses they will strew the way,

Chorus
Get ready for the Jubilee,
Hurrah! Hurrah!
We'll give the hero three times three,
Hurrah! Hurrah!
The laurel wreath is ready now
To place upon his loyal brow

Chorus
Let love and friendship on that day
Hurrah! Hurrah!
Their choicest treasures then display
Hurrah! Hurrah!
And let each one perform some part
to fill with joy the warrior's heart

Chorus

Parades

A parade is an organized group of people who march down the street to celebrate an event or special occasion. Sometimes parades include animals or floats. They almost always include colorful costumes and music from a marching band. Some parades are held for religious purposes. Other times, they are held to honor a person, group of people, or an entire city. You can find a parade in almost every American city on July 4th each year.

In the 1920s, immigrant employees at Macy's department store in New York City decided to stage a parade resembling those they had loved in Europe. They marched in costume down the city streets, accompanied by bands and live animals borrowed from the Central Park Zoo. Large balloons first appeared in the parade in 1927. After the parade, they were let go and would float for days. The lucky finder was awarded a prize!

The Rose Parade, held on New Year's Day in Pasadena, California, began in 1890 with horse-drawn carriages covered in roses. People new to the West Coast held the parade to celebrate their region's mild winter. Now the parade features motorized floats covered in thousands of flowers. These floats sometimes take a year to design and create!

Different cultures hold parades for different events. Mexican Americans march in parades, sometimes dressed as skeletons, to celebrate El Dia de los Muertos (Day of the Dead) on November 2nd. Irish Americans celebrate St. Patrick's Day on March 17th with a parade featuring bagpipers. Participants tend to wear green. Chinese New Year, held in January or February, is a fifteen-day celebration ending with children carrying lanterns in a parade featuring a large dragon.

Make Your Own Parade Instruments

It's easy to make your own parade instruments with a few household items. Choose one of the three designs below. Make your own instrument, and then have a classroom parade!

Kazoos

Materials: cardboard toilet paper roll or paper towel roll cut in half, one piece of waxed paper 5 inches (12.70 cm) square, rubber band, markers and stickers for decorating

Directions: First, decorate the cardboard roll with markers. You can add your favorite patriotic symbols or other symbols to show what America means to you. Then, place a square of waxed paper around one end of the cardboard roll and slip the rubber band around it to hold it in place. Now you can hum or sing your favorite patriotic tunes into the open end of your kazoo.

Drum

Materials: Empty oatmeal box or other cylindrical cardboard container with lid, colored paper, tape, markers

Directions: First, tape a piece of colored paper around your box and color it with markers. You can color your box to look like a drum, or decorate it with your favorite American symbols. Put the lid on your box, and you're ready to set the beat for a marching tune! Don't forget the drumsticks. Try pencils, dowels, or use your hands.

Guitar

Materials: Shoebox with no lid, colored paper, tape, markers, six rubber bands

Directions: Tape a piece of colored paper to your shoebox and color it with markers. You can decorate your box to look like a guitar, or color it with your favorite images of America. Then, pull all six rubber bands carefully over the box, spacing them evenly across the open end. Now you can strum out a spiritual or other American song.

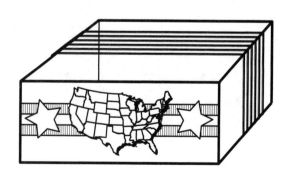

Yankee Doodle

Everyone knows the song "Yankee Doodle," but no one knows who wrote it. Most musical historians agree that it was composed in the 1750s. The Dutch called New Englanders "Yankees." A "doodle" was another word for a "fool."

In 1755, a British solider sang the song while he was making fun of tired, dirty American soldiers who fought with the British against the French and the Indians. "Macaroni" referred to the tall hairstyles that fashionable people in London wore. The British soldier was making fun of Americans, joking about how they were so foolish that they thought a feather was "macaroni."

He also said that the Americans would be so frightened by the war cannons that they'd run home to their mothers.

Twenty years later, American soldiers fighting in the Revolutionary War sang "Yankee Doodle" as they marched into battle against the British. Bands played it at sites of victory, and "Yankee Doodle" became our first unofficial national anthem. People began calling all Americans "Yankees."

After you have read and discussed the words of "Yankee Doodle" as a class, answer the questions below.

1. Define the following words from "Yankee Doodle":

   handy _____

   hasty pudding _____

   stallion _____

   troopers _____

   deuced _____

   scamper _____

2. What did the narrator see when he went to camp with his father?

   _____

   _____

3. How does he describe George Washington?

   _____

4. What does the narrator do at the end of the song?

   _____

Yankee Doodle

by Anonymous

Yankee Doodle went to town,
A-riding on a pony,
Stuck a feather in his cap
And called it macaroni.

> *Chorus:*
> *Yankee doodle, keep it up,*
> *Yankee doodle dandy;*
> *Mind the music and the step,*
> *And with the girls be handy.*

Father and I went down to camp,
Along with Captain Gooding;
And there we saw the men and boys,
As thick as hasty pudding.

> *Chorus*

There was Captain Washington
Upon a slapping stallion,
A-giving orders to his men,
I guess there was a million.

> *Chorus*

The troopers, too, would gallop up
And fire right in our faces;
It scared me almost to death
To see them run such races.

> *Chorus*

And then we saw a swamping gun,
Large as a log of maple;
Upon a deuced little cart,
A load for father's cattle.

> *Chorus*

And every time they shoot it off,
It takes a horn of powder;
It makes a noise like father's gun,
Only a nation louder.

> *Chorus*

Uncle Sam came there to change
Some pancakes and some onions,
For lasses cake to carry home
To give his wife and young ones.

> *Chorus*

But I can't tell you half I saw
They kept up such a smother;
So I took my hat off, made a bow,
And scampered home to mother.

> *Chorus*

Flags and Ribbons

The Earth Flag

The Earth Flag is a symbol of global and environmental awareness. It was created in 1969 by John McConnell. The first photographs of Earth, taken by men on the Apollo 11 Space Mission, inspired this flag. It has been presented to United States presidents and leaders all over the world. The Earth Flag flies at the United Nations, the Mir Space Station, and the North and South Poles. To see photos of it, go to the website below:

http://www.earthflag.net

Ribbons

People have been wearing ribbons to symbolize mourning or political protest for centuries. During the War of 1812 and the Civil War, women braided ribbons into their hair until their soldiers returned from battle. Red ribbons signified mourning for those soldiers missing in action in both World Wars. In 1980, Americans were taken hostage in Iran. People began to wear yellow ribbons in support of their release. They sang the popular song, "Tie a Yellow Ribbon Round the Old Oak Tree" and tied yellow ribbons on trees and streetlights. Now, people wear different colored ribbons to symbolize their support for a variety of causes.

Match the Color with the Cause

Go to the following website and answer the questions below:

http://rampages.onramp.net/~arthur/ribbons/

1. Name one thing that pink ribbons stand for:

   _____

2. Name one thing that orange ribbons stand for:

   _____

3. What color ribbon would you wear if you love chocolate?

   _____

Make a Peace Windsock

Design and create a windsock to symbolize your feelings about peace. When you have completed it, hang your windsock in the classroom or at home.

Materials:

- red and white crepe paper streamers
- blue construction paper, 9 x 18 inches (23 x 46 cm)
- glue, stapler, scissors, tape
- white chalk or silver glitter
- yarn or string

Directions:

1. Think about what pictures symbolize peace for you. Use white chalk or glue and glitter to make these pictures on the blue paper.

2. Form the blue construction paper into a cylinder.

3. Glue the shorter side closed. Staple it to make sure it doesn't come undone.

4. Attach red and white streamers to one end with glue.

5. Cut three 12-inch (30.5 cm) lengths of string. Tape them to the top of the blue cylinder, about six inches (15 cm) apart.

6. Knot the three strings together to make a hanger.

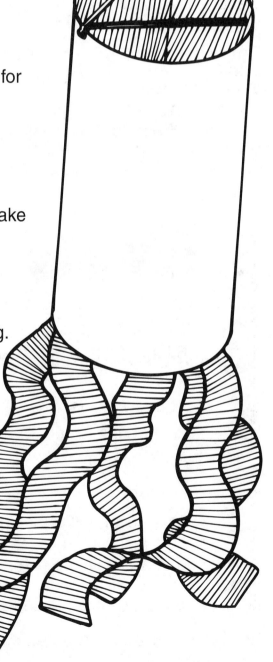

Johnny Appleseed

Johnny Appleseed (1774–1845) symbolizes those Americans who first ventured into the western part of the United States. He was an American pioneer born in Massachusetts. Johnny's real name was John Chapman. In the early 1800s, he traveled west, planting apple seeds all the way. He dedicated his life to planting and nurturing apple seedlings in Ohio, Indiana, and Illinois. He also gave away thousands of these seedlings to other settlers.

Legend says that Johnny traveled barefoot. One of his friends said the skin on his feet was so thick that it would kill any rattlesnake that tried to bite his foot. He wore ragged clothes and a tin pot as a hat. Johnny never stayed long in one place. His cooking equipment consisted of a camp kettle, a plate, and a spoon. He slept on a bed of leaves or the ground, with his feet near the campfire for warmth.

Johnny was said to be a kind and generous man who loved nature and the Native Americans. He got along well with the different tribes, as well as with settlers moving in from the East. Johnny Appleseed Day is celebrated on March 11th. You might want to eat an apple, or even plant an apple tree, in Johnny's honor!

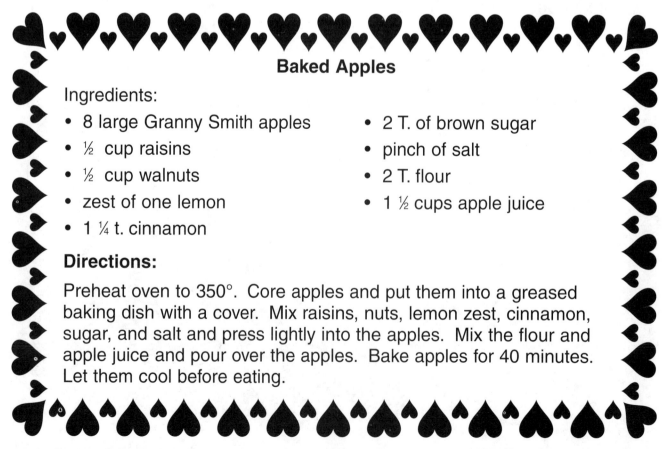

Baked Apples

Ingredients:

- 8 large Granny Smith apples
- ½ cup raisins
- ½ cup walnuts
- zest of one lemon
- 1 ¼ t. cinnamon

- 2 T. of brown sugar
- pinch of salt
- 2 T. flour
- 1 ½ cups apple juice

Directions:

Preheat oven to 350°. Core apples and put them into a greased baking dish with a cover. Mix raisins, nuts, lemon zest, cinnamon, sugar, and salt and press lightly into the apples. Mix the flour and apple juice and pour over the apples. Bake apples for 40 minutes. Let them cool before eating.

Symbols on Money

Have you ever really looked at the back of a one-dollar bill? If you have, you'll notice that it's full of symbols! For instance, both sides of The Great Seal of the United States can be found on this bill. The back side of this seal shows a

pyramid with an eye on top of it. The eye symbolizes the all-seeing eye of Divine Providence. The front of the Great Seal of the United States shows a bald eagle holding arrows in one talon to symbolize war and an olive branch in the other talon to symbolize peace. If you turn a one-dollar bill over, you'll see the first President of the United States, George Washington, in the center. There are olive branches around the outside of this bill.

Now look at a penny. On the front of this coin, you'll see a picture of Abraham Lincoln with the word "Liberty" to his left. The words "In God We Trust" run across the top of the penny. This is our official national motto. It has appeared on all American currency since Congress approved it in 1955. If you turn a penny over, you'll see a picture of the Lincoln Memorial. This is a national monument that was dedicated to Abraham Lincoln in 1922. Above the Memorial, you'll find the Latin words *E Pluribus Unum.* They mean "Out of many, one." These words appear on almost every American coin and bill.

Currency Search

Materials: a variety of coins and bills

Directions: Choose one coin or bill. Examine it. Then answer the questions in the space below. For help understanding the symbols on the currency you've chosen, you can go to the website:

http://www.frbsf.org/currency/iconography/plants.html

1. Whose portrait do you see on the front of the coin or bill you've chosen?

_____

_____

2. What words appear on the front of this coin or bill? What do they mean?

_____

_____

3. What objects appear on the back of your coin or bill? What do they symbolize?

_____

_____

4. What words appear on the back of your coin or bill? What do they mean?

_____

_____

5. **Extra credit:** What does the date on the front of your coin or bill mean?

_____

_____

Design Your Own Money

What would you put on a coin and a bill to symbolize your feelings about America? In the spaces below, design both sides of a coin and a bill. Have fun!

Symbols on Stamps

You can often find symbols on postage stamps. For instance, American postage stamps have featured The Statue of Liberty, the United States flag, and the American bison (also called the buffalo).

The idea for postage stamps was first suggested by a British teacher named Rowland Hill in 1837. In 1840, the first postage stamp was released in England.

It cost a penny and featured a picture of Queen Victoria. The United States came out with its first postage stamps in 1847. Benjamin Franklin appeared on the five-cent stamp. The ten-cent stamp showed a picture of George Washington. Since then, American presidents, and other people who have made important contributions to our society, have appeared on postage stamps. However, pictures of living people are forbidden!

Some people love to collect postage stamps from around the world. This hobby is called philately. Stamps can be symbols of our history, politics, geography, art, music, and other parts of civilization.

Adventures with United States Stamps

Materials: Stamps of several monetary values

Directions: Choose two stamps from the selection given. In the space below, draw each stamp. *Below your drawing*, write in the name of the person or object that appears on this stamp. Then explain what this person or object symbolizes.

_____   _____

_____   _____

Research Other Countries' Currency and Stamps

Most countries in the world have their own currency and stamps. Do some research on the Internet or in an encyclopedia to answer the questions below.

1. Choose one foreign coin or bill. Draw a picture of both the front and the back of this currency in the space below.

2. What country uses this coin or bill? _____

3. What symbols do you see on the front and back of this currency?

   _____

---

1. Choose one foreign stamp. Draw a picture of the stamp in the box to the left.

2. What country uses this stamp?

   _____

3. Who or what is on the front of this stamp? _____

   _____

4. How does this person or object symbolize the country? _____

   _____

   _____

Write a Class Song

You have learned many songs in this book which describe America. Now, think about what objects, emotions, and people best describe your class. Answer the questions below. Then help your teacher to write a class song on the chalkboard.

1. What feelings do you have when you walk into your classroom each morning? _____

   _____

2. What do you like best about your class? _____

   _____

3. Describe one fun time you've had in your class. _____

   _____

4. Describe some of the kids in your class. _____

   _____

5. Describe your teacher. _____

   _____

6. What would you like other classrooms to know about your class?

   _____

   _____

Copy your class song from the chalkboard in the space below.

_____

_____

_____

_____

_____

_____

_____

_____

National Symbols Riddles

Directions: Use words from the glossary below to answer the following National Symbols Riddles.

Glossary of National Symbols

U.S. Flag	"The Star-Spangled Banner"
Statue of Liberty	Donkey and Elephant
Pledge of Allegiance	Bald Eagle

1. I am the promise that Americans make to be loyal to our country.
   What am I? _____

2. I symbolize the Democratic Party. What am I? _____

3. I symbolize the Republican Party. What am I? _____

4. I was given to the United States by France. Now I stand in the New York Harbor. What am I? _____

5. I am the national anthem. What am I? _____

6. I am called "Old Glory." What am I? _____

7. I am seen as a symbol of freedom, courage, and strength. What am I?

   _____

Patriotic Stationery

Choose a border from the three below to duplicate at the top of plain or lined paper for a letter to your congressperson, as suggested on the following page.

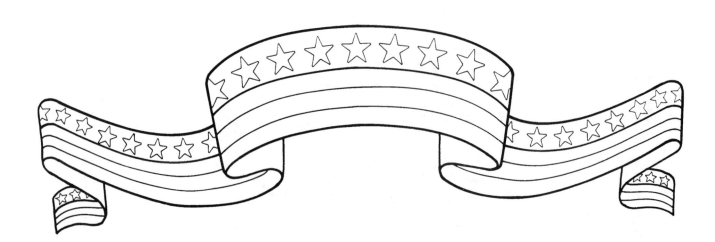

Write to Your Congressperson

Your senator and state representatives want to hear from you. You can often find their names and addresses in the government pages in your phone book. Use the form below as a sample of how to write a letter to a government official. You might thank the official for his or her hard work, mention something you love in the United States, or express concern about problems you see in your community.

Senator Mary Mills
United States Senate
Washington, DC 20510

July 4, 2002

Dear Senator Mills,

I am writing to say thank you for your hard work. My mother told me that you love nature. She said that you are working to keep our air and water clean.

I love nature, too. I really like to hike in clean air and have clean water to drink. My friends and I pick up trash when we find it.

Thank you again for your help.

Sincerely,

Jonathan Smith

Answer Key

Page 6

1. **Definitions**

   perilous-dangerous

   ramparts-protective barriers

   gallantly-bravely; courageously

   dread-a great fear that something might happen

   reposes-to lie at rest; absence of activity

   fitfully-restlessly; convulsively

   desolation-empty, barren wasteland

   preserved-saved, kept

   motto-a saying that expresses what is important to a state, nation, family or group.

2. the American flag
3. to preserve American freedom
4. The Americans who gained freedom from Great Britain.
5. It honors those people who fought to make American a free nation, and we still value their courage and dedication.

Page 9

1. fifty
2. answers will vary
3. answers will vary
4. 37
5. answers will vary
6. 117

Page 10

1. **Definitions**

   grand-great

   emblem-sign or symbol

   boast-to praise oneself; to brag

   brag-to praise oneself; to boast

   acquaintance-friend

2. It has been around for a long time.
3. Americans are brave, free, and humble.
4. Cohan means old friends. He could mean that if we forget our relationship to our country, we should look at the flag to remember.

Page 16

1. **Definitions**

   spacious-roomy; vast

   amber-light brownish-yellow

   brotherhood-a close feeling between people

impassioned-showing intensity of feeling

thoroughfare-a way of passage

liberating-setting free

strife-conflict

divine-sacred or holy

patriot-a person who loves, supports and defends his or her country

alabaster-a kind of smooth stone, sometimes carved for decoration.

2. the majestic view from Pike's Peak; fields of fruit trees
3. They moved from England to America to start a new country.
4. They are the people who fought to keep American free. She admires their courage and dedication.

Page 18

1. 2080 lbs.   2. London
3. It cracked.   4. 1752
5. in a glass pavillion near Independence Hall

Page 20

1. **Definitions**

   native-inborn, natural

   noble-having or showing qualities of high character

   rills-small brook

   rapture-being carried away by overwhelming emotion

   mortal-certain to die someday

   partake-take part; share

   prolong-to continue; to lengthen

2. The men who helped make America an independent nation.
3. rocks, hills, trees
4. We should sing of our happiness at being a free country.

Page 27

1. Give matches to an adult; don't throw cigarette butts; never leave a campfire unattended; keep a bucket of water and a shovel near a campfire.
2. 1. Dig a pit away from overhanging branches.
   2. Circle the pit with rocks.
   3. Clear a 5-foot area around the pit down to the soil.

4. Stack extra wood upwind and away from fire.
5. After lighting, do not discard match until cold.
6. Never leave a campfire unattended.
7. Keep a bucket of water and shovel nearby.

Page 30

1. **Definitions**

   hearty-unrestrained, vigorous, with strong feeling

   peal-loud ringing of bells

   lads-boys

   lassies-girls

   strew-spread all over

   jubilee-season of celebration

   laurel-crown of honor

   choicest-best

2. Any soldier fighting for American freedom.
3. Because he has survived the war.
4. They will throw rose petals, cheer, shout, ladies will turn out, sing, have a parade, and ring the church bells.

Page 34

1. **Definitions**

   handy-useful; convenient

   hasty pudding-corn meal mush; porridge of oatmeal

   stallion-male horse

   troopers-soldiers

   deuced-tricked

   scamper-run about quickly and playfully

2. He saw guns, soldiers, and George Washington.
3. He's giving orders upon a "slapping stallion."
4. He gets scared and runs home to his mother.

Page 36

1. Breast cancer; Princess Diana
2. Families with a loved one in prison; youth suicide prevention
3. Brown

Page 45

1. Pledge of Allegience
2. donkey
3. elephant
4. Statue of Liberty
5. Star-Spangled Banner
6. American flag
7. bald eagle